‹ ISRAEL ›

MAJOR WORLD NATIONS

ISRAEL

Mary Jane Cahill

CHELSEA HOUSE PUBLISHERS
Philadelphia

Chelsea House Publishers

Contributing Author: Stephen Holzman

Copyright © 1999 by Chelsea House Publishers,
a subsidiary of Haights Cross Communications.
All rights reserved.
Printed and bound in Malaysia.

3   5   7   9   8   6   4

Library of Congress Cataloging-in-Publication Data

Cahill, Mary Jane.
Israel.
Includes index.
Summary: Surveys the history, topography, people, and culture
of Israel, with emphasis on its current economy, industry,
and place in the political world.
ISBN 0–7910–4742–3
1. Israel. [1. Israel.]
I. Title.
DS102.95.C34   1988
956.94   87–18252
CIP

◄ CONTENTS ►

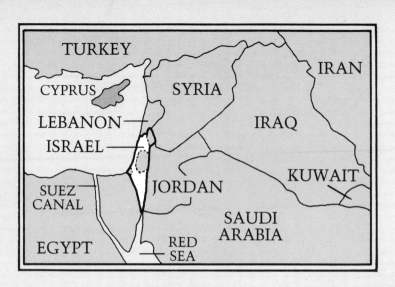

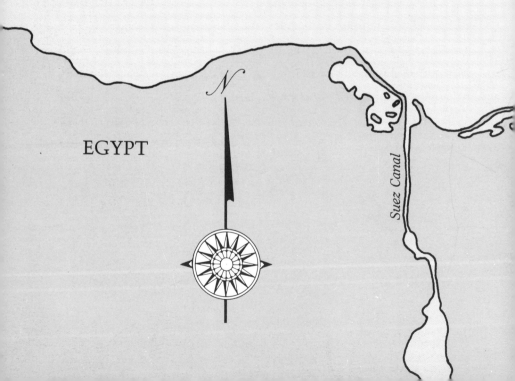

MEDITERRANEAN
SEA

EGYPT

N

Suez Canal

◄ FACTS AT A GLANCE ►

Area	7,990 square miles (20,700 square kilometers)
Highest Point	Mt. Meron (3,963 feet, or 1,208 meters)
Population	5,619,000
Population Density	703 people per square mile (271 per sq km)
Capital	Jerusalem
Major Cities	Jerusalem, Tel Aviv, Haifa, Beersheba
Official Languages	Hebrew, Arabic
Other Languages	English is the most common second language
Religions	Jewish, 83 percent; Muslim (mainly Sunni), 13 percent; Christian (mainly Greek and Roman Catholic), 2.5 percent; Druze and other minority religions, 1.5 percent

Economy

Major Products	Citrus fruits, vegetables, processed foods, cut diamonds, metal products, fertilizers, chemicals, textiles, electronics and high technology
Gross Domestic Product	$80.1 billion
Economic Sectors	Public services, 33 percent of gross domestic product; commercial services, 27 percent; industry, 22 percent; transportation and communications, 8 percent; construction, 7 percent; agriculture, 3 percent

Currency   New Israeli shekel

Average Annual Income   Equal to U.S. $18,360

Government

Form of Government   Democratic republic; legislative power rests with the one-chamber, 120-seat parliament, called the Knesset; executive power rests with the cabinet, headed by a prime minister

Head of State   President, elected by the Knesset to a five-year term

Head of Government   Prime Minister, elected by the majority party in the Knesset

Voting Rights   All citizens over 18 years of age

Political Subdivisions   Six administrative districts

◄HISTORY AT A GLANCE►

2000 to 1700 B.C.	Abraham leads his people to Canaan. Because of famine, Abraham's grandson Jacob leads the Hebrews to Egypt.
1300 to 1260 B.C.	Moses leads the Jews out of Egypt.
1020 B.C.	Saul becomes the first king of the Hebrews.
1000 to 961 B.C.	King David consolidates much of the kingdom of Israel.
961 to 922 B.C.	King Solomon expands the kingdom's borders and builds the First Temple.
922 to 722 B.C.	Political fighting splits the country into the kingdom of Israel and the kingdom of Judah.
722 B.C.	The Assyrians conquer the kingdom of Israel; Jews living there are killed or deported; they become known as the 12 "lost" tribes.
586 B.C.	Babylonians capture Judah, destroy the temple, and remove most Jews to Babylon.
539 B.C.	Jews return to Judah and rebuild the temple.
during 300s B.C.	Alexander the Great conquers the territory; his rule is displaced by the Egyptians.
198 B.C.	Antiochus IV of Syria conquers Judah and tries to destroy the Jewish religion.
142 B.C.	The Jews under Judas Maccabaeus revolt and regain control of Judah.
63 B.C.	Civil war weakens the Jewish state; the Roman general Pompey takes over the country.

70 A.D.	Under the leadership of the Zealots, some Jews revolt against Rome. Roman legions destroy Jerusalem and the temple.
73	Zealots commit suicide at Masada.
135	Romans deport almost all Jews from Palestine. The Diaspora begins.
395 to 638	The Byzantine Empire rules Palestine and imposes Christianity on the region.
641 to 1072	Arab Muslim armies take Jerusalem and rule Palestine.
1090	Christian Crusaders capture Jerusalem.
1187	Saladin recaptures Jerusalem for the Arabs.
1291	The Egyptian Mamluks defeat the last of the Crusaders. Palestine remains under their rule for several centuries.
1516	The Turkish Ottoman Empire conquers Palestine.
1300 to 1600	Jews living in Europe are persecuted and killed; many are wrongly blamed for causing the bubonic plague, which kills millions during the Middle Ages.
1881 to 1891	Jews from Poland, Russia, and Romania emigrate to Palestine to escape persecution.
1917	Britain captures Palestine from the Turks during World War I. Britain issues the Balfour Declaration, which supports a Jewish home in Palestine.
1921	Palestinian Arabs riot to protest continuing Jewish immigration.
1922	The League of Nations puts Palestine under British administration.
1939	Britain restricts Jewish immigration and land purchases.

1947   Britain turns over the issue of the settlement of Palestine to the United Nations (UN); the UN calls for the division of Palestine into Jewish and Arab states.

1948   On May 14, Israel proclaims itself an indepenent state. On May 15, the armies of Egypt, Syria, Lebanon, Iraq, and Jordan invade Israel, beginning the first Arab-Israeli war.

1956   Israel, Britain, and France attack Egypt after Egyptian president Gamal Abdel Nasser nationalizes (claims ownership of) the Suez Canal. The United States and other nations condemn the attack. After two months, the United Nations negotiates a cease-fire.

1967   The Six-Day War begins on June 5, when Israel attacks Egypt. At the war's end, Israel has gained the Sinai Peninsula, the Golan Heights, the Gaza Strip, and the West Bank territories.

1973   Egypt and Syria attack Israel on Yom Kippur, a Jewish holy day, beginning the October War. The war lasts for more than two weeks, until the United Nations negotiates a cease-fire.

1977   Egyptian president Anwar Sadat flies to Jerusalem to "break down the walls" that divide his nation and Israel.

1979   Egypt and Israel sign a peace treaty on March 26. Egypt recognizes Israel and Israel returns the Sinai Peninsula to Egypt.

1981   Israel annexes (claims as part of its country) the Golan Heights, which it had seized during the Six-Day War.

1982   Israel returns the Sinai Peninsula to Egypt. In June, Israeli troops invade Lebanon and lay siege to Beirut. In August, the United Nations oversees the evacuation of Syrian and Palestinian fighters trapped in West Beirut.

A Jewish immigrant family from Algeria arrives in Haifa.

1983   Prime Minister Menachem Begin resigns.

1984   Labor party and Likud bloc form national unity
        government; Israel assists immigration of
        Ethiopian Jews.

1985   Israeli troops withdraw from Lebanon.

1987   Palestinian *intifada* (uprising) starts in Israeli-
        administered territories.

1989   Four-point peace initiative proposed by Israel.
        Mass immigration of Jews from Soviet Union be-
        gins.

1991   Israel attacked by Iraqi Scud missiles during
        Gulf War. Middle East peace conference con-
        vened in Madrid.

1992   Diplomatic relations begin with China and India.
        Yitzhak Rabin of the Labor party heads new gov-
        ernment.

1993   Israel and Palestine Liberation Organization
        (PLO) sign declaration of principles on self-
        government for Palestinians.

1994   Palestinian self-government begins in Gaza Strip
        and Jericho. Israel-Jordan peace treaty is signed.
        Yitzhak Rabin, Shimon Peres, and PLO leader
        Yasir Arafat are awarded the Nobel Peace Prize.

1995   Prime Minister Rabin is assassinated by a Jewish
        assailant. Shimon Peres becomes prime min-
        ister.

1996   Benjamin Netanyahu is elected prime minister,
        and the Likud party forms a new government.

This is all that remains of a fort built by the Crusaders 1,000 years ago in Caesarea.

Israel and
the World

The Middle Eastern nation of Israel has been in the news since the day it became an independent country in 1948. Several wars and countless acts of terrorism have focused the world's attention on this small, triangular state. Only the United States and the now-disbanded Soviet Union have had a larger impact on international politics in the last several decades.

Perched on the eastern edge of the Mediterranean Sea, modern Israel has special significance for two of the world's largest religions—Islam and Christianity. But it is the followers of Judaism, one of the world's oldest religions, who have laid special claim to Israel.

The Jews first settled in what is now Israel in around 2000 B.C. For more than a thousand years they endured invasions and civil strife, only to be persecuted and expelled by armies of the Roman Empire in 135 A.D. Living in exile in all parts of the world, the Jews found hope in the belief that one day they would return to their former homeland. For centuries this hope seemed futile because the land that the Jews once claimed had passed into the hands of a new people, the Arabs, and had become known as Palestine. By the late 19th century, however, Jews began returning in small numbers to Palestine. Over the next 50 years, the work of Zionists (Jews around the world devoted to creating a Jewish nation) and the tragedy of the Holocaust (the slaughter of millions of Jews by Germany during World War II) led to the creation of the state of Israel.

Today, Israel is the newfound home of a million Jews from around the world. These immigrants have turned deserts into farmland and have created sprawling cities out of tiny, dusty villages. A vibrant, democratic government provides strong leadership and allows each Israeli a voice in guiding the country's future.

But many problems confront Israel. Economic problems, such as a trade deficit, plague the country. Internal conflict and violence are caused by ethnic divisions between Oriental Jews and European Jews, religious divisions between Orthodox (very religious) Jews and

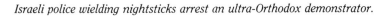

Israeli police wielding nightsticks arrest an ultra-Orthodox demonstrator.

secular (nonreligious) Jews, and, most important, political divisions between Jews and Arabs.

Israel continues to seek solutions to problems with the Palestinians, the Arab inhabitants of the territory that became Israel in 1948. Since that year, the Palestinians have struggled to regain their homeland. The Israelis have also had to fight neighboring Arab nations, and political terrorism has become all too common. In the past decade, Israel has broadened the series of peace initiatives that began with its landmark peace treaty with Egypt in 1979. Yet the solutions call for concessions by both sides, and factions within Israeli society and among the Palestinians remain opposed. As a result, the tension and violence that have beset the region since the start of the Zionist movement continue.

Rapid changes have occurred in Israel's half-century of independence. They are the result of the Israeli people's determination to build a new nation that would be unique among the countries of the world. Israel's uniqueness comes not only from recent developments there, but from its history as well.

Israel's rich history ensures it a special place among the world's nations. From the modern skyscrapers of Tel Aviv one can see the crumbling ruins of castles built in the Middle Ages by the Crusaders. The tombs of biblical figures such as Abraham and Sarah cast their afternoon shadows over the same dusty plains that Alexander the Great crossed on his way to conquer Asia.

The past will continue to play an important role in Israel. This is especially true in the conflict between the Israelis and the Palestinians. The Israeli and Palestinian claims to the same land are rooted in the past; perhaps from out of the past a just and lasting solution will be found to the conflict between these two peoples.

These Hebrew costumes date back to antiquity.

The Chosen People

The long history of Israel and its people begins with the birth of Western civilization. Long before its explosive politics made headlines, Israel was at the heart of some of the world's most important events.

Most of our knowledge about Israel's early inhabitants comes from the Old Testament of the Bible. Although not all of the Bible's stories have been confirmed by historians, many of its accounts of these first inhabitants—known as the Hebrews—correspond to archaeological evidence that has been found in the region over the years.

The first Western civilization began only a few hundred miles east of modern Israel, where the Tigris and Euphrates rivers meet in what is now the nation of Iraq. This area, once called Mesopotamia (Greek for "land between two rivers"), was settled by the Sumerians, an advanced people who established the first written language and laid the foundations of modern mathematics and astronomy. In 2000 B.C., invasions from the west and northeast destroyed the Sumerians and led to the beginning of the first Jewish state.

At the time of the Sumerian destruction, a seminomadic people (that is, a people who did not settle in a village but who moved often in order to find pasture for their livestock) lived in Haran in Mesopotamia. Their leader was Abraham. According to Genesis, the first book of the Bible, God told Abraham to lead his people to the neighboring country of Canaan (now the site of Lebanon and Israel). God and Abraham made a covenant (agreement); Abraham promised to believe and obey God, and God promised to protect Abraham and his people in their new home in Canaan. Abraham and his followers journeyed to this "Promised Land," where they continued their life of herding cattle, sheep, and goats. The Canaanites called Abraham and his people *habiru,* the Canaanite word for wanderers. Over time, Abraham's people became known as "Hebrews."

About 1700 B.C., drought and famine caused Abraham's great-grandson, Joseph, to lead the Hebrews to Egypt. At first the Egyptians welcomed the Hebrews, but within a few years the Egyptian pharaoh (ruler) had forced them into slavery.

The Hebrews remained in bondage for almost 400 years, building the pharaoh's pyramids and longing to return to Canaan. In 1300 B.C., Moses, one of Judaism's greatest prophets, rallied the Hebrews and persuaded the pharaoh to allow them to return to Canaan. (According to the Old Testament, Moses had received signs that he was chosen by God to lead the Hebrew people back to the Promised Land.)

The return to Canaan took 40 years. During this time, Moses and the Hebrews pledged themselves to worship only one God and to obey his laws. In return for this loyalty, the Bible says, God made the Hebrews his "chosen people" and promised them that Canaan would become "a land flowing with milk and honey."

Unified in their belief in one God, the Hebrews—who now called themselves the nation of Israel, or Israelites—entered Canaan. But they met resistance from the native Canaanites, and a long series of battles followed. By the 11th century B.C., the Israelites had defeated the Canaanites and had gained control over much of the country.

Soon, however, a new foe appeared. A people known as the Philistines settled on the coast of Canaan. Equipped with iron weapons, the Philistines quickly became a threat to the Israelites. In the face of this threat, the 12 Israelite tribes decided to form a loose confederation and choose a king who, according to the Bible, "may govern us and go before us and fight our battles." In 1020 B.C., the Israelites named Saul the first king of Canaan.

Saul was known for his military exploits against the Philistines, and he expanded the kingdom. But it was his heir, David, who gave the Israelites a national identity and transformed Canaan into a wealthy, politically powerful state. Born in Bethlehem, which was then as now a dusty town on the far outreaches of the capital city of Jerusalem, David came to King Saul's court as an aide. He later married Saul's daughter, Michal, and became a great warrior, famous for his military exploits against the Philistines.

When Saul was killed in a battle with the Philistines in 1000 B.C., the Israelites proclaimed David king. During his reign, David unified the Hebrew people, joining the 12 tribes into a nation based on a shared religion. King David also forced the Philistines back to a narrow strip on the Mediterranean coast of Canaan.

Solomon's Reign

After King David died in 961 B.C., his son, Solomon, became king. Solomon dominated Canaan and the surrounding region and turned Canaan into a commercial center that traded in arms and food. He erected forts and cities throughout Canaan. With King Hiram of Tyre in neighboring Phoenicia, he sent ships on expeditions throughout the Red Sea and the Indian Ocean. He lavished particular attention on his capital city, Jerusalem, building a royal palace and immense city walls.

Solomon's most important undertaking was building a temple in which the Israelites could worship their God. Called the First

Temple, it became the central shrine of the Hebrews and the most important building in the country. For more than seven years, 70,000 men worked on the building of the First Temple, creating a marvel of ivory-paneled doors, bronze pillars, golden vessels, and carved statues.

Solomon's grand designs came at a high price. He forced Hebrew men to build his palaces and the temple, and he made the people pay huge taxes to support the royal court's life-style and the temple's expensive ornamentation. When Solomon died in 922 B.C., discontent over his policies erupted into open rebellion.

Canaan's ten northern tribes demanded that the new king, Solomon's son Rehoboam, reduce taxes and end forced labor. Rehoboam refused, saying he would impose even harsher requirements: "My father made your yoke heavy; I will make it heavier."

Rehoboam's harsh response was a fatal political error. The ten tribes withdrew from the central government and formed their own nation, the kingdom of Israel. Rehoboam was left to rule the southern kingdom, which became known as Judah.

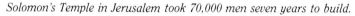

Solomon's Temple in Jerusalem took 70,000 men seven years to build.

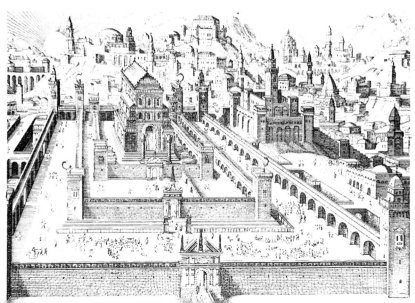

Although the new kingdom of Israel was prosperous, it did not have a strong, stable government. (In its two centuries of existence, it was ruled by 19 kings.) In 722 B.C., the army of the neighboring kingdom of Assyria captured Israel and deported its people. The kingdom was destroyed, and the fate of these ten "lost tribes" became a mystery.

Judah withstood the Assyrian threat and continued to thrive. But it was not strong enough to resist the armies of King Nebuchadnezzar of Babylonia, a country in Mesopotamia. In 586 B.C., Nebuchadnezzar captured and burned Jerusalem, reducing Solomon's temple to rubble. Almost all the Israelites were taken captive and sent to Babylonia.

The captive people of Judah, now called the Jews, were exiled in Babylonia for more than 40 years. In 539 B.C., Cyrus the Great of Persia conquered Babylonia and gave the Jews permission to return to Judah. The 40,000 people who chose to return rebuilt Jerusalem and constructed the Second Temple.

But the Jews who returned did not rebuild Judah's strong government or empire. Their country remained under Persian control until it was conquered by Alexander the Great of Macedonia in 332 B.C. Afterwards, control of Judah fell to the Ptolemies, Egyptian descendants of one of Alexander's generals. They ruled until 198 B.C., when Antiochus IV of Syria captured Judah from the Ptolemies.

Unlike the Persians, Macedonians, and Egyptians who had ruled before him, Antiochus tried to suppress the Jewish religion. His soldiers killed hundreds of Jews and defiled their temple, carting off its riches. The Jews revolted. In 142 B.C., a rebellion led by Judas Maccabaeus defeated the Syrian army and regained Judah's independence.

Judah was again an independent kingdom, but corrupt leadership soon led to civil war among the Jews. In 63 B.C., two brothers each claimed to be king. In a fateful step, they agreed to ask Pompey the Great, one of the leaders of the powerful Roman Empire, to settle the question of who should be king. Pompey consented to their request. He marched his Roman legion into Jerusalem and claimed it—and all Jewish territory—for the Roman Empire. The civil war between the brothers ended, and Roman rule began.

Memories of Empire

For the next 300 years, the Roman Empire ruled Judah, which it called Palestine. The Romans appointed puppet kings and governors to carry out the imperial government's wishes. One of these governors was Pontius Pilate, who tried and sentenced Jesus Christ.

As the years passed, the Jews grew unhappy with Roman rule. In 66 A.D., the Zealots, a band of Jewish nationalists (Jews who believed the Jewish territory should be independent) staged a rebellion. Using guerrilla tactics, the Zealots terrorized the Roman legions. In 70 A.D., Roman legions under the command of Titus, the son of the Emperor Vespasian, destroyed Jerusalem and demolished

Titus celebrated his victory over Judea with a Triumph, or procession. In 70 A.D., Titus ordered the destruction of Jerusalem and the Second Temple.

The mountaintop fortress of Masada was built by King Herod. It was here that a band of Jewish nationalists made a last stand and committed mass suicide in 73 A.D.

the Second Temple, leaving standing only one wall, known today as the Wailing Wall.

A band of Zealots fled to Masada, a mountaintop fortress that had been built by King Herod, a ruler installed by Rome. The Zealots were besieged in Masada by Roman legions for two years. When the Romans finally managed to mount a final assault in 73 A.D., the Zealots committed suicide in order to keep their enemy from achieving final victory. Many modern Israelis consider this mass gesture of defiance the greatest moment in the history of the Jewish people.

Jewish revolts occurred again in 115 and 132. In 135, Rome decided to prevent any more rebellion. It destroyed the city of Jerusalem and plowed up the ground on which it stood. Thousands of Jews were killed. Most of the survivors were enslaved and sent to Rome's colonies. A few fled to Europe and North Africa.

During the next 1,700 years, several empires ruled the land that Judah had occupied. After razing Jerusalem, the Romans showed little interest in the province, which they called Palestine. In the 3d and 4th centuries the Roman Empire began its long process of decline as German tribes beat back the Roman legions in the western half of the empire and marched on Rome. The eastern half of the Roman Empire, especially the city known as Byzantium (now Istanbul, Turkey), withstood the barbarian attacks, however, and in 324 the Byzantine leader Constantine became emperor of the entire empire.

Constantine moved the capital of the Roman Empire to Byzantium (which became known as Constantinople after his death). A pagan who had converted to Christianity, Constantine promoted the Christianization of the Roman Empire. Constantine died in 337, and in 395 the Roman Empire officially split into two empires: the Western Roman Empire and the Eastern, or Byzantine, Roman Empire.

Palestine fell under the control of the Byzantines, who turned many of the sites where Jesus Christ had lived or performed miracles into shrines. Churches were built in Jerusalem and in other areas of western Palestine, and some of the area's inhabitants converted to Christianity.

In 614, Persian armies under the command of Khosru II swept into Palestine and captured Jerusalem from the Byzantines. Within a few years, however, the Byzantine emperor Heraclius had destroyed the Persian armies and, in 628 he recaptured Jerusalem. But Heraclius's rule over Palestine was short-lived. Thirteen years later, a new band of invaders from the East captured Jerusalem and the surrounding region.

These new invaders, who traced their ancestry to the nomadic tribes of the Arabian peninsula, called themselves Arabs. The Arabs had lived on the peninsula, in what is now Saudi Arabia, for centuries, but it was only in the 7th century that they developed a powerful and unified army. The reason for this unification—and for the Arab invasions of neighboring lands—was the new religion of Islam.

In 641, an Arab army led by Omar, the second caliph (Arabic for "successor") of the Muslim empire, captured Jerusalem from the Byzantines. For the next 400 years, the Arabs ruled Palestine. They gradually turned the country into an Arabic, Islamic land. The Muslims (followers of Islam) built mosques (places of worship) and shrines throughout the land, especially in Jerusalem. They revered Jerusalem as a holy place because Muhammad dreamed he ascended to heaven from this city.

Islam considers Christianity and Judaism fellow religions; that is, Christians and Jews believe in the same God that Muslims do, although their other beliefs and practices differ. The Muslims thus allowed the Christians and the few Jews in Palestine to practice their faiths unhindered. However, Jews and Christians did not have the same political rights as the Muslims, and they were required to pay higher taxes. The Muslim Arab population began to grow. Soon it was the largest group in Palestine.

In 1095, the Christian nations of Europe mounted the first of several crusades to "rescue" Jerusalem and the Holy Land from the Muslims. The Crusaders considered the Muslims infidels (enemies of the faith) who were occupying and desecrating the holy places of Christianity. The Crusaders fought their way to Palestine and captured Jerusalem in 1099. A Crusader at the capture of the city described it this way:

> Wonderful sights were to be seen . . . . Piles of heads, hands, and feet [covered] the streets of the city . . . . It was a just and splendid judgment of God that this place should be filled with the blood of the unbelievers, since it had suffered so long from their blasphemies.

The Crusaders built castles throughout the country, which they called the Latin kingdom of Jerusalem. In 1187, Saladin, the sultan (leader) of Egypt and Syria, recaptured Jerusalem for the Muslims. The Christians launched a new crusade, led by Richard the Lion-Hearted of England, to expel Saladin's Muslim armies. After years of fighting, the Crusaders finally accepted a truce, and Saladin agreed to allow Christians to visit the shrines and churches of Jerusalem.

After the truce, Saladin's attention shifted to the east as Mongol armies began to invade Iraq. The task of removing the remaining Crusaders in Palestine and restoring Muslim rule in the region fell to the Mamluks, Egyptian slaves who had converted to Islam and had become fierce warriors. In 1291, the Mamluks ejected the last of the Crusaders who had held out in isolated areas of Palestine. The next two centuries of Mamluk rule was uneventful, and Palestine sank into the same medieval bleakness that covered Europe at the time.

In 1516, Mamluk rule was abruptly ended by the powerful armies of the Turkish Ottoman Empire that would rule Palestine for the next 400 years. They were followers of Islam who created an empire that stretched from Algeria to Austria. The Ottomans divided their large empire into provinces, each ruled by a governor who was appointed by the caliph in Constantinople. Palestine became one of the provinces and was ruled according to Ottoman law. Arab Muslims were not allowed to hold government posts, but they had rights that were denied to Jews and Christians, who were treated as second-class citizens; for example, Jews and Christians were not permitted to ride horses or carry weapons.

The Ottomans paid little attention to Palestine. The province was a land of a few large Ottoman-owned estates and many small farms and villages. In 1801, Napoleon of France landed a force of troops at Gaza, the former Philistine stronghold on the Mediterranean coast of Palestine. Napoleon hoped to move east and conquer all of Asia. A joint British and Ottoman force defeated Napoleon, and Palestine again sank back into obscurity until it became a pawn in the battles fought between the Turks and the British in World War I (1914–1918).

The war had a dramatic effect on Palestine. Palestinian Arabs and other Arabs throughout the Middle East fought with British forces in hopes that they would defeat the Turks and gain independence for Palestine. By the end of the war, the Turks had been defeated and driven out of Palestine. But the British, who had taken control of Palestine, did not grant it independence at the war's end because another group of people demanded a say in its government: the Jews.

Theodore Herzl (1860–1904), a Hungarian-born Austrian writer, founded the Zionist movement. Zionism brought thousands of Jews to Palestine.

The Birth of Israel

After the Romans destroyed Jerusalem in 135 and deported almost all the Jews living in Palestine, the Jews spread to countries throughout the world. Those living outside Palestine were said to be in the Diaspora, from the Greek word meaning "to be dispersed" (spread out).

The number of Jews in the Diaspora grew over the centuries. Some Jews became rich and prosperous; many others were persecuted and murdered. Some Christians believed that Jews were responsible for the bubonic plague that ravaged Europe in the Middle Ages. From the 13th to the 16th centuries, Jews who lived in Christian Europe were systematically hanged, burned, or expelled. Returning to Palestine became a universal theme for all Jews; "If I forget thee, O Jerusalem, let my right hand forget her cunning," became a part of many Jews' prayers, and "Next year in Jerusalem!" became their New Year's wish.

In the 18th century, some Jews did return to Palestine, which was then part of the Ottoman Empire. In 1775, a large migration of Jews occurred. In 1839, a band of Hasidim, members of an extremely religious Jewish sect, also migrated to Palestine. Most of these early immigrants lived in Jerusalem.

In the late 19th century, European anti-Semitism (persecution of Jews) convinced many Jews that they needed their own country in order to be safe. One of the leading proponents of the belief that Jews needed a homeland was Theodore Herzl. Through his books and speeches, Herzl, an Austrian Jew, helped create the Zionist movement, an organization of Jews who called for large-scale migration to Palestine and economic aid for the new settlers.

The Zionist movement was successful. Between 1882 and 1914, thousands of Russians, Polish, and other East European Jews made aliyah—Hebrew for returning to Palestine—to escape pogroms (massacres) and government restrictions on the rights of Jews. By 1914, 85,000 Jews were living in Palestine. These early settlers spoke Hebrew and established farms throughout the country. On November 2, 1917, the Zionist cause received a major boost. British Foreign Secretary Arthur Balfour sent a letter to Zionist leaders declaring that Great Britain supported "the establishment in Palestine of a national home for the Jewish people."

The Balfour Declaration, as it came to be known, took on added significance at the end of World War I, when Germany and its ally, Turkey, were defeated. Turkey, which had ruled Palestine for centuries, was stripped of its colonies at the end of the war. The League of Nations, an international peacekeeping organization similar to today's United Nations, granted Great Britain a mandate (the right) to govern Palestine and help guide it to independence. The Balfour Declaration was made part of the mandate.

British support for Zionism elated the Jews but angered the Arabs, who had lived in Palestine for more than 1,000 years and who now made up 90 percent of the population. The Palestinians argued that since they were the majority and had lived in the country continuously since the 7th century, they should be allowed to form an independent government. In 1920 and 1921, some Palestinians rioted to protest Jewish immigration.

The British responded to the Arab riots. In 1921, the British high commissioner for Palestine, Herbert Samuels, temporarily restricted Jewish immigration. In 1922, a group of British officials headed by Winston Churchill issued a document that said the Jews had a right to live in Palestine, but that this did not mean Palestine should be only a Jewish state; Arabs, too, had a right to live there. Churchill's group also limited the area Jews could live in by putting what is now Jordan off limits to Jewish migration.

Nevertheless, Jews continued to pour into Palestine. As the number of Jews in Palestine increased, the Palestinians became angrier. Responding to their complaints, the British set rigid quotas on the number of Jews who could enter Palestine. Despite the quotas, by the late 1930s Jews made up 30 percent of Palestine's total population. These Jewish immigrants established an official defense force, a legislature, more than 200 Zionist farming settlements, and some entirely Jewish cities and towns.

In 1939, the British decided to permit only 75,000 more Jews to enter Palestine in the next five years—after that no more Jewish immigration would be allowed. Many Jews feared that this meant the end of the Jewish state. But the Holocaust—Nazi Germany's attempt to exterminate the Jews of Europe—set in motion events that would result in an independent homeland for the Jews.

The Second Exodus

Between 1936 and 1939, thousands of Jews fled Germany to escape from Adolf Hitler's Nazi movement. Hitler was a virulent anti-Semite who encouraged anti-Semitism and violence against Jews. In 1935, his Nazi party created the Nuremberg Laws, which deprived Jews of German citizenship and their civil rights. After Germany launched World War II in 1939, the Nazis rounded up Jewish men, women, and children and sent them to concentration camps, where they were tortured and murdered.

By the time the war ended in 1945, six million Jews from all over Europe had been murdered in the Nazi death camps. (The Allies—the countries that opposed Germany in the war—did not know the actual number of Jews killed until after the war, but they did know during the war that German, French, Dutch, Polish, Italian, and Russian Jews were being deported to concentration camps and were being murdered there.) Many of the Jews who escaped from Europe wanted to go to Palestine, but Great Britain refused to raise its quota to allow Jewish refugees to settle there.

The Jews in Palestine reacted to Britain's restrictions by organizing a massive "underground railway," similar to the one that helped escaped slaves leave the southern United States before the American Civil War. Some 10,000 European Jews used safe houses and secret contacts to move from city to city and country to country until they secretly entered Palestine. Jews living in Palestine also joined forces with the British and fought against the Germans in battles across North Africa.

At the end of World War II, the British declared that only 1,500 European Jews could enter Palestine each month, and that all Jewish immigration was to stop after 150,000 Jews had entered. This move satisfied neither the Jewish settlers nor the original Arab inhabitants: the Zionists wanted to bring the rest of Europe's Jews to Palestine; the Palestinians wanted no more Jews to come.

Radical Zionists decided to take up arms to force the British to allow more immigration. Three underground Jewish armies—the Haganah and the much more violent Irgun and Stern Gang—sabotaged British installations, ambushed military caravans, and engaged in terrorism in an attempt to convince Great Britain to change its policies. The British army responded to the violence with force, and the dead and injured on both sides began to number in the hundreds. Underground Palestinian Arab groups also fought against both the Jews and the British in Jerusalem and throughout the country.

In order to end the violence, Great Britain asked the United Nations to take authority over Palestine. On August 31, 1947, the United Nations recommended that Britain give up its mandate and that Palestine be partitioned (separated) into two independent but economically linked Jewish and Arab states. It also proposed that Jerusalem be declared an international city claimed by neither Arabs nor Jews. On November 29, 1947, the United Nations voted 33 to 13 in favor of the partition (10 nations did not vote).

The neighboring Arab states—Egypt, Syria, Lebanon, Iraq, and Transjordan (now called Jordan)—closed ranks and declared their disapproval of the partition. Although war had not been officially declared, thousands of guerrilla soldiers from surrounding Arab countries entered Palestine and attacked Jewish settlements.

War and Uneasy Peace

On May 14, 1948, Britain's mandate over Palestine ended. The British high commissioner left and the state of Israel officially declared its independence. Before independence, the Israelis had already formed civil defense forces and a militia; 60,000 men stood ready to defend

These emaciated survivors of the Nazi concentration camp at Evensee, Austria, were rescued by the U.S. Third Army in 1945.

In prewar Palestine, a British policeman searches an Orthodox Jew for weapons.

the new nation. But the army did not have enough weapons to equip all its soldiers, and those it had were not as powerful as the weapons used by the Arabs states. The United States recognized the new state immediately, but refused to provide it with arms.

On May 15, 1948, the armies of Syria, Lebanon, Egypt, Iraq, and Jordan invaded the new Jewish state. War raged until January 7, 1949, when the United Nations Security Council brought an end to hostilities.

Israel not only survived the war, but also expanded its borders beyond those originally drawn up by the United Nations. It now included the city of Jaffa, near Tel Aviv, the new city of Jerusalem (distinct from the old, walled city of Jerusalem, which remained in Jordanian hands), and a corridor of land from Jerusalem to the Mediterranean Sea.

In May 1949, Israel became the fifty-fourth member of the United Nations. Creating a strong country now became the Israelis' main task. New immigrants began to arrive in large numbers. The

Israelis built roads and encouraged new industries. They undertook dramatic experiments in agriculture and irrigation and reclaimed huge areas of desert for farming. On January 29, 1949, Israelis went to the polls for the first time and elected a legislature.

For the next seven years, Israel was at peace with its neighbors. Then, in October 1956, Egyptian President Gamal Abdel Nasser nationalized the Suez Canal (declared it to be part of Egypt). This canal, which had been built by the French in the 19th century, was owned by Britain and France and was an important route for international cargo ships. In retaliation for Nasser's action, France and Britain sent military forces to seize the canal, starting a war with Egypt. Israel, which had suffered attacks from guerrillas based in Egypt, secretly agreed to join with the British and French and send its troops into Egypt's Sinai Peninsula. The United States, the Soviet Union, and the Arab nations all criticized this British-French-Israeli attack on Egypt.

In December, the United Nations halted the war and stationed an emergency force in the Gaza Strip (a strip of coastline around the city of Gaza) to maintain order. The Egyptians reopened the canal (which they had blocked during the fighting), and the Israelis withdrew from the Gaza Strip in March of 1957.

For the next ten years, Israel experienced a period of relative peace. But in 1966 and 1967, tensions increased between Israel and Syria, which is located on Israel's northeastern border. Guerrilla raids from Syria and retaliatory military strikes by Israel became more frequent. In May 1967, to show support for Syria, Egyptian President Nasser ordered the UN troops out of the Gaza Strip and the Sinai Peninsula and moved in 80,000 of his own soldiers. Egypt then blocked Israeli shipping. On May 30, Jordan and Egypt signed a mutual defense pact.

On June 5, after all-day artillery duels with Syria and Egypt, Israel attacked Egypt. Within one hour, Israel had destroyed the

Egyptian air force and sent the infantry across the Sinai Peninsula. Then it began fighting with Syria and Jordan.

In six days the war was over. The Israeli troops had quickly overrun the Arab forces. Once again, Israel had enlarged its borders through warfare. It now occupied Egypt's Sinai Peninsula and the Gaza Strip, Syria's Golan Heights region, the West Bank of the Jordan River (part of Jordan), and, most important, the old city of Jerusalem.

In November 1967, the United Nations Security Council adopted a resolution calling for peace in the Middle East. Resolution 242 called for each state in the region to acknowledge the integrity and independence of the others and to refrain from threats and acts of war. It also called for Israel to return the occupied territories to its Arab neighbors. The Israeli government said it would not return the territories until all the Arab states formally recognized Israel, and in 1969 Israeli Jews began building settlements in the occupied areas.

Israel was in a strong position after the Six-Day War, but it still had to contend with the root of Arab hostility—the homelessness of the Palestinians. During the 1960s, Palestinians began forming groups aimed at gaining back the land they had lost. Some groups sought to regain the land through political means; others used terrorism. One group, the Palestine Liberation Organization (PLO), became quite powerful. After the Six-Day War, the PLO began staging terrorist attacks and hijacking airplanes to publicize its cause. One of its bloodiest attacks occurred in September 1972, when PLO terrorists killed 11 Israeli athletes at the Olympic Games in Munich, West Germany.

Meanwhile, Syria, Jordan, and Egypt vowed to recapture the territories they had lost to Israel in the Six-Day War. On October 6, 1973—Yom Kippur, or the Day of Atonement (the holiest of all Jewish holidays)—Syrian and Egyptian troops attacked Israel on separate fronts. Although the Arab forces won major victories at first, the Israelis quickly recovered to beat back the Egyptian and Syrian advances and push the Arab forces into their home territories.

On October 24, Syria, Egypt, and Israel agreed to a cease-fire, to be supervised by the United Nations. In 1974, renewed peace efforts led Israel to pull back its forces from the Suez Canal and to return the canal to Egypt.

In 1977, the troubled politics of the Middle East entered a new era when an Arab nation stepped forward to make peace with Israel. On November 19, Egyptian President Anwar Sadat flew to Jerusalem to meet with Israeli Prime Minister Menachem Begin. Sadat said it was time to "break down the walls" that separated Israel and Egypt. At long last, peace seemed possible.

Egyptian president Anwar Sadat arrives in Jerusalem for his historic speech before the Knesset. Behind his left shoulder is Menachem Begin.

After their meeting in Jerusalem, Begin and Sadat accepted United States president Jimmy Carter's invitation to hold peace talks at the president's retreat at Camp David. During the talks, Begin and Sadat agreed on several issues that had divided the two countries. Egypt agreed to recognize Israel's right to exist and to establish diplomatic relations; Israel agreed to return the Sinai Peninsula to Egypt. On March 26, 1979, the two leaders signed a peace treaty in Washington, D.C.

But peace between Israel and Egypt did not end the Palestinians' struggle for a homeland, and terrorist attacks by the PLO and other radical Palestinian groups continued. Many of these attacks were launched from Lebanon, where hundreds of thousands of Palestinians had settled. In 1982, Israel decided to try to end the PLO's attacks by destroying its bases in Lebanon. Thus began one of the most disturbing wars in Israel's history.

The Struggle Continues

The invasion of Lebanon offset the progress toward peace made at Camp David. A siege by Israelis of Beirut, where Palestinian and Syrian fighters were entrenched, was lifted when the PLO evacuated the city. A month later, Christian Lebanese allied with Israel massacred hundreds of Palestinian men, women, and children. Israeli outrage over the massacre led to the resignation of Prime Minister Begin, but Israel did not manage to withdraw from Lebanon until 1985.

The strife between Palestinians and Israelis was aggravated by triple-digit inflation and the expansion of Israeli settlements in the Occupied Territories. Relations deteriorated to a low point in 1987, when Palestinians in the West Bank and Gaza began a series of often violent strikes and demonstrations called the *intifada*, or uprising. Complicating the pressures on Israeli society was the need in 1990 to assimilate some 350,000 immigrants from the Soviet Union, which was in the process of breaking up. A year later, in an effort to gather Arab support for his policies, Iraqi president Saddam Hussein ordered Scud missile attacks against Israel as an international coalition of armed forces moved to expel his army from Kuwait. The damage to Israel was mostly psychological. However, it led many Israelis to believe that peace efforts should be intensified, while others became even more determined to resist concessions to the Arabs.

The 1990s produced several milestones along the path to peace: a Middle East peace conference in 1991, a peace treaty with Jordan in 1994, and the establishment of contacts with Morocco, Tunisia, Oman, Qatar, and Bahrain. Most noteworthy was the signing in 1993 by Israel and the PLO of a Declaration of Principles that outlined arrangements for Palestinian self-government in the West Bank and Gaza Strip. With this came a pledge by the PLO to renounce terrorism and set aside the articles of its covenant denying Israel's right to exist. In response, Israel recognized the PLO as the representative of the Palestinian people.

But progress continues to encounter roadblocks. The peace process was fundamentally altered in 1995 with the assassination of Prime Minister Yitzhak Rabin, a Labor party moderate, by a Jewish opponent of the peace initiatives. In the wake of this event, the conservative Likud party, which has historically taken a harder line toward compromise, returned to power. In 1996, attacks by the Islamic militant group *Hezbollah*, or Party of God, on communities in northern Israel led to Operation Grapes of Wrath, in which Israeli Defense Forces pursued and attacked Islamic fighters in southern Lebanon, causing more civilian casualties. As these events demonstrate, the pursuit of peace remains a difficult struggle.

Lake Tiberias is one of the most popular vacation spots in Israel.

A Land of Contrasts

Every visitor to Israel is a time traveler. Stand on Mount Nebo, overlooking the Dead Sea, and gaze at the Judean Hills as Moses did thousands of years ago when he realized he would not live to lead his people into the Promised Land. Pace the shores of the Sea of Galilee, where the followers of Jesus Christ anxiously waited for a storm to pass. Read the inscription two Roman soldiers carved into a paving stone in Jerusalem in 70 A.D., when Imperial troops arrived to destroy the city: "To Marcus Janius Maximus, Legate of the Emperors in command of the Tenth Legion Frentensis Antoniana, by Caius Domitius Seriganus and Julius Honoratus, his equerries."

This land, where the past is still present, is an oddly tilted triangle that comprises 7,990 square miles (20,700 square kilometers). It is bordered on the north by Lebanon, on the northeast by Syria, on the east by Jordan, on the south by Egypt, and on the west by the bright blue Mediterranean Sea. Its southernmost tip dips into the Gulf of Aqaba, which flows into the Red Sea. North to south, it is 256 miles (412 km) long; east to west, it is 21 miles (33 km) at its widest. Its Mediterranean coastline is 143 miles (230 km) long.

Israel is a land of stark geographic contrasts. In only a few hours, one can travel from blistering desert to fertile farm valley and then to a chilly mountaintop that slopes downward to a staggering 400 feet (121 meters) below sea level. Israel has four distinct geographic regions: the narrow coastal plain, the Galilean-Samarian-Judean Highlands, the Negev Desert, and the Jordan Rift Valley.

The coastal plain extends 117 miles (187 kilometers) along the Mediterranean coast, providing Israel with some of the most dramatically beautiful white-sand beaches in the world. At its broadest, near the Gaza Strip, the coastal plain is 30 miles (48 km) wide. It is known by various names throughout the country. North of Haifa, it is called the Plain of Zebulun; from Haifa to Tel Aviv, the Plain of Sharon; and south of Tel Aviv, it is called the Plain of Judea.

Except for the sandy beach and dune area of Tel Aviv, the coastal plain has been a fertile farming ground for centuries. The heart of the country's citrus farms, it contains some of the largest, most successful agricultural settlements in the country.

Two kinds of thick, sedimentary river deposits form the soil of most of the coastal plain. One is dark and heavy, which is ideal for growing field crops; the other is thin and sandy, providing an excellent soil for citrus. Because the soil and weather are perfect for crops, Israeli farmers use far fewer chemical fertilizers and pesticides than farmers in other parts of the world; this gives their fruits and vegetables a distinctive, delicious taste.

Only two significant rivers cross the coastal plain: the Yarkon, which is 26 miles (42 kilometers) long and flows from the Judean Hills near Jerusalem into the Mediterranean, and the 27-mile- (43-km-) long Kishon, which flows into the Gulf of Acre near Haifa. Because the rivers are so small, most water for drinking and irrigation must come from wells.

Besides being the country's most fertile region, the coastal plain is also the most populated. Two-thirds of Israel's population lives on the plain. Major coastal cities include Haifa, Israel's chief port; Tel Aviv, the most populous city; and Ashdod, the end point for an important oil pipeline. Despite the long coastline, however, there are few natural harbors large enough for tankers or container ships.

The second geographic region is the Galilean-Samarian-Judean Highlands. These highlands are ranges of hills that stretch from Galilee in the north to the Judean Hills in central Israel. Jesus Christ lived most of his life in the Galilean region. He was born in the town of Nazareth, now a bustling, traffic-clogged city where many of the nation's Arabs live. The highest mountain in Israel, Mount Meron (3,962 feet, or 1,208 meters) looms over Galilee. The western slopes of the Galilean Highlands are, on average, 2,000 feet (610 meters) above sea level. Here, small fertile valleys dotted with orchards and vineyards nestle between gently rolling highlands. Farming can be difficult because of sudden, crop-destroying winter frosts. The eastern slopes of the Galilean Highlands are rugged, with deep, impassable valleys and sparse vegetation.

The central section of the highlands is a mountainous area known as the Samarian Hills. It includes Mount Carmel, near Haifa; the Plateau of Dalia to the southeast; and Mount Gilboa. The Judean Hills, on which Jerusalem is built, form the southern portion of the highlands. These steep, rocky hills are covered with green trees and an abundance of wildflowers.

The third geographic region is the Negev Desert, which is actually the eastern portion of Egypt's Sinai Desert. It extends from the Gulf of Aqaba in the south to the city of Beersheba, the chief city of the region and an important industrial center. A low mountain chain runs across the northern section of the desert from northeast to southwest. Its highest elevation is Mount Ramon (3,396 feet, or 1,035 meters).

The Negev Desert is monotonously flat and incredibly hot. Unlike the sandy Sahara, with its mountainous dunes, the Negev has a dusty, windblown surface made of hardpan gravel. At the desert's extreme southern end is the small resort town of Elat, a favorite spot for swimming and sunbathing. Elat's beaches are made of stone rather than sand, but the colorful variety of fish and plant life in the Red Sea more than makes up for the painful walk to the surf.

West of Beersheba, at the northwestern border of the Negev, is the Beersheba basin. Although the basin holds great potential for agriculture because of its fine-grained soil, called *loess*, it receives only about 8 inches (203 millimeters) of rainfall annually. The Israelis have begun cultivating sections of the basin by pumping in water from the Sea of Galilee in the north through an 88-mile (142-kilometer) system of canals, pipelines, and tunnels called the National Water Carrier.

Israel's fourth and most dramatic geographic region is the Jordan Rift Valley, part of a geographical trench known as the Great Rift Valley that stretches from Syria to Mozambique in southern Africa. The steep, rocky Jordan Rift Valley runs along Israel's eastern border. Its northern section includes the Jordan River, whose waters were used by 1st-century Christians to baptize followers. The Jordan River flows south from Syria's Golan Heights for 157 miles (253 kilometers) until it empties into the Dead Sea. The Jordan's path forms the border between Jordan and the occupied West Bank. The river is not navigable, and at times it is no wider than a small stream.

The Sea of Galilee (also known as Lake Tiberias or Lake Kinneret) is also located in the northern valley. A freshwater lake covering 64 square miles (166 square kilometers), it is the most popular vacation spot in Israel. Motorboats towing waterskiers cruise its perimeters, and the shoreline is usually packed with campers.

South of the Sea of Galilee, the valley's geography becomes harsh. Green banana plantations tucked into the shadow of the Golan Heights slowly give way to desolate, dry, rock-hard soil. Bedouins (nomadic Arabs) graze their camels and livestock on the few blades of scrub grass that manage to survive. This desolate portion of the valley plunges downward until it reaches 1,300 feet (396 meters)

The fortress-like stables in this tiny settlement in the Negev show that the settlers are prepared to defend themselves against attack.

below sea level, the lowest point on land anywhere in the world. To the west of the valley lies the Israeli-occupied West Bank, to the east lies Jordan, and in the center of the valley lies the Dead Sea.

The Dead Sea

The body of water known as the Dead Sea is actually a landlocked lake fed by the Jordan River. It is 46 miles (74 kilometers) long and 10 miles (16 km) wide. The waters of the lake are 2 percent salt— three times as salty as ocean water. The water's salt content is so high that bodies float on its surface and cannot sink. The high salt content means fish and vegetation cannot live in the Dead Sea; only simple, salt-loving microorganisms can survive.

Most people who visit the Dead Sea immediately stick one of their fingers into the oily looking water and pop it into their mouths—no one ever asks for a second taste. Exposure to the Dead

Sea's potent minerals can open up a freshly healed flesh wound or make a recent one fester and refuse to close. Swimming is out of the question: the water causes eyes to sting, tongues and lips to swell, and skin to itch unbearably.

Although it is useless for irrigation or recreation, the Dead Sea has tremendous commercial value. Israel extracts huge quantities of

salt and minerals from it. Potash, magnesium, and bromine—used in making dyes and pharmaceuticals—are removed at sophisticated chemical plants. Scientists have also discovered that Dead Sea algae can be converted into petroleum. Israel, which has no oil deposits, hopes to find an economical way to extract the petroleum.

Engineers are working to replenish the sea's water level, which

The Dead Sea has considerable commercial value for Israel, which extracts large amounts of salt and minerals from it.

is slowly dropping because of changes in the climate and the diversion of the Jordan River's water for farming. They plan to dig a long channel from the coast that would allow water from the Mediterranean Sea to flow into the Dead Sea.

Looming high over the sea is Masada, the scene of the Zealots' mass suicide in 73 A.D. In the distance one can also see the ancient city of Jericho. Along the northwestern side of the sea rise cliffs filled with caves; it was in these caves that the Dead Sea scrolls—ancient copies of the books in the Hebrew Bible—were discovered in 1947 by a young Bedouin boy.

Weather and Wild Things

Israel's climate in most regions is ideally suited for agriculture, which forms a major part of the country's economy. The country has two seasons: summer, which lasts from April to October, and winter, from November to March. Temperatures are warm during the summer, reaching highs of 82° Fahrenheit (29° Centigrade) along the coast. Temperatures in the Negev, the central mountains, and the Jordan Rift Valley are also warm in the summer, but the humidity is much lower than in the coastal region.

Winter is the most popular time for tourists to visit Israel. During the winter months, the climate is more temperate than during the summer. In January, temperatures in Jerusalem might dip as low as 43° F (6° C); the average daily temperature in Tel Aviv in January is 56° F (13° C).

Most rainfall occurs during the winter months. The average rainfall along the coastal plain in Tel Aviv is 21 inches (533 millimeters). Farther inland the rainfall increases but in the south, toward the Negev, it decreases. Elat receives an average of only 1 inch (25.4 mm) of rainfall per year. The Jordan Rift Valley is also extremely dry, and its average annual rainfall of 15 inches (381 mm) quickly evaporates.

Centuries ago, Israel's mountains were covered by forests. But overgrazing and the use of the trees for lumber and firewood have destroyed most of the country's vegetation. Some species of brush and shrub have survived, however, among them the Aleppo pine, the Tabor oak, and the evergreen oak. In the late 19th century, Jewish settlers began a vigorous policy of reforestation that continues today; at present there are 300,000 acres (120,000 hectares) of forest.

Israel is a bird-watcher's paradise. Hundreds of varieties of rare birds can be spotted even in the crowded housing developments around Jerusalem. There is also a wide variety of animals, including hyenas, jackals, otters, lynx, leopards, gazelles, porcupines, mongooses, wolves, and weasels. The government has established game preserves to protect the wildlife population and repopulate the country with rare species.

Israel has a population of 5.6 million people, 83 percent of whom are Jewish.

Israeli Society

When Israel declared its independence in 1948, the Zionist dream of an independent homeland for Jews became a reality. The country immediately opened its doors to all Jews living in the Diaspora. In the next twenty years, more than 700,000 Jews from all over the world flowed into the country.

With their conflicting ideas about government, religious practices, education, culture, and even food, these immigrants have made Israel an enormous melting pot of people and cultures. Sometimes the pot bubbles over, but, for the most part, this nation of immigrants is unified in its support of the state of Israel.

Israel has a population of 5.6 million people, 83 percent of whom are Jewish. Of these, 50 percent are native-born Israelis (called Sabras); the rest are from some 70 countries in Europe, the Western Hemisphere, and Asia or Africa. The two main Jewish ethnic groups are the Askhenazim. Jews of European descent, and the Sephardim, or so-called Oriental Jews, who are from the countries of the Near East and the Mediterranean basin, such as Turkey, Iran, and Morocco.

Almost all of Israel's non-Jews (about 17 percent of the population) are Arabs. About 77 percent of the non-Jews are Muslims;

about 14 percent are Christians; and 9 percent are Druzes (members of a mystical religious sect with beliefs that are derived from Islam) or members of other religions.

Hebrew and Arabic are both official languages, but Hebrew is the dominant language. English is a required language for Israeli students and is spoken as a second language.

An Evolving Culture

The first Zionists wanted to create a Jewish nation free of the middle-class traditions of Europe. Except for an appreciation of music and literature, which they refused to surrender, these pioneering Zionists discarded the formalities of middle-class culture. Those who complain about poor food in Israeli restaurants should remember that the elaborate, formal cuisine of Western Europe was one of the first traditions abandoned by the Zionists. Food in Israel, they believed, should be only plainly cooked meat, potatoes, and vegetables.

As the years pass, however, tastier food is making its way onto Israeli menus. Arabic food, which is flavorful and spicy, is a popular alternative. Israelis are welcome at many Arab-owned restaurants and cafes. When Jewish restaurants in Jerusalem close on Friday night for the Jewish Sabbath, many Jews who are not strictly religious drive to East Jerusalem, an Arab neighborhood, to eat Arabic foods such as lamb, *hummus* (mashed chickpeas with lemon and garlic), and sandwiches made of falafel (a spicy vegetable mixture that is rolled into balls and fried).

Besides hummus and falafel, Israelis eat many other Arabic foods. Light sandwiches made of pita bread (flat bread shaped into round, hollow loaves) and tahini (sesame seed paste) are popular. A heavier sandwich of sliced, spicy lamb stuffed into pita bread is called *shwarma*.

Most Israelis eat these sandwiches after a light breakfast of tomato, cucumber, radish, and scallion salad, topped with lemon oil

(continued on page 65)

SCENES OF
ISRAEL

◄ *A tourist explores the ruins of a Roman ampitheatre in Caesarea.*

⋁ *The Negev Desert is flat and hot, with steep sand dunes and a surface made of hardpan gravel.*

◄ *An Arab suq, or bazaar, is filled with tiny shops selling souvenirs, trinkets, clothing, and food.*

◄ *Little has changed in the streets of Nazareth since the birth of Jesus.*

▼ *Kibbutzniks gather for their communal dinner.*

▲ *These Bedouins (desert-dwelling Arab nomads) are engaged in deep conversation at a market.*

➤ *The Israeli Philharmonic is conducted by Zubin Mehta, who was also music director of the New York Philharmonic until 1991.*

▲ *The harbor at Haifa, a busy coastal city 60 miles north of Tel Aviv, is Israel's main deep-sea port.*

A group of folk dancers performs in traditional costumes in Haifa.

◄ *The white sandy beaches, such as this one at Tel Aviv, are very popular with natives and tourists alike.*

Y *The famous King David Hotel is surrounded by picturesque churches and a mosque.*

▲ Muslims believe that Muhammad ascended to heaven from the site on which the Dome of the Rock mosque was built.

➤ Like this couple, many visitors to the Dead Sea enjoy floating on its salt-laden waters.

(continued from page 56)

and salt and eaten with a piece of pita bread. Another breakfast food is *leban,* an Arabic yogurt similar to plain yogurt but slightly more sour.

The main meal of the day is lunch, which may be a dish of *babaganoush,* made from roasted eggplant mixed with garlic, tahini, and lemon juice. Eggplant is a widely used food and is prepared in a variety of ways. A light dinner of salad or fish is usually eaten after seven o'clock in the evening.

The early Zionists rejected formal Western dress, and even today most Israelis wear casual clothes. Men never wear neckties or suit jackets—even to weddings or funerals—and women dress in cotton dresses or in pants. For the most part, people walking on the streets of Tel Aviv, Haifa, or the new city of Jerusalem wear the same Western fashions that can be found in Athens, Beirut, and other Mediterranean cities. However, some Israelis wear their own distinctive dress. For example, many older Arab men still wear *kaffiyehs,* red-and-white or black-and-white checked headdresses that are held in place by braided headbands.

Although the early Zionists attempted to build a Jewish state with its own characteristics, Western culture is not shunned in Israel. Most Israelis wear Western clothes, listen to Western music, and have, in general, adopted Western life-styles. American culture especially has had an enormous impact on Israel, so much so that some Israelis consider Israel the "fifty-first state."

American popular music is heard throughout the country, and several radio stations play only "top 40" hits. The large classical music audience can listen to concerts performed by the Israeli Philharmonic Orchestra, which is conducted by Zubin Mehta, who also conducts the New York Philharmonic Orchestra.

Many of the world's greatest musicians were born in Israel, including the violinists Pinchas Zukerman and Itzhak Perlman. Almost every town and agricultural settlement has a small chamber orchestra or ensemble. Folk dancing based on the heritage of many of the immigrant groups is also popular, and nightclubs that specialize in presenting these dances are always crowded.

Israel has more libraries than any other country in the Middle East: 1,000 libraries with more than 10 million books. Israelis also buy large numbers of books, and more than 3,000 books and pamphlets are published every year on a variety of subjects. A large number of newspapers and magazines provide reading material on a daily, weekly, and monthly basis.

More than 100 museums are located throughout the country. The Israel Museum in Jerusalem houses relics from King Solomon's reign and from the Roman legions; the Dead Sea scrolls and other biblical treasures can also be found there. The Bezalel Museum, also in Jerusalem, is devoted to arts and crafts, and the Billy Rose Garden, named for a New York theater producer who donated many of the artworks, contains modern sculptures. Jerusalem has many gardens, libraries, and theaters that have been donated by Jews living outside Israel.

Israelis are avid theatergoers. Theater productions range from classical to contemporary works. Children's theater is especially popular, and roving acting troupes perform in kibbutzim (cooperative farm settlements) and small settlements around the country.

Israeli film companies make movies that have been critically acclaimed throughout the world. Israelis also flock to movie theaters to see American, British, French, and Italian films with Hebrew subtitles.

Ethnic Conflict

When Israel became a state in 1948, the majority of the Jews in the country were Ashkenazic (European). Since the late 19th century, the Ashkenazim had worked to build the foundations of a Jewish state. They had created a government, begun the first economic enterprises, and sparked the cultural and intellectual life of the country. Most of the Askhenazim were highly educated, and, with some exceptions, championed Western European culture and values.

After 1948, however, large numbers of Sephardic (Oriental) Jews began pouring into the country. Although many Sephardim were highly educated, the majority were not. Most had lived in small villages scattered throughout North Africa and were unfamiliar with the life-styles and culture of the European Jews. Conflicts between the two groups began almost immediately and continue today.

The Ashkenazim came to Israel driven by the Zionist dream of a Jewish state based on socialism and democracy. Moreover, the Ashkenazim had been persecuted in their homelands and believed that only in Israel could the Jewish people find safety and political freedom. The Sephardim, on the other hand, saw Israel more in religious terms. For them, Israel was Geullah, or delivery from exile and return to the Promised Land, and going to Israel was the fulfillment of biblical prophecy. The Sephardim put less emphasis on the political aspects of Israel than did the Ashkenazim.

An Ashkenazi Jew at home. Since the late 19th century, the Ashkenazim have worked to build the foundation of the Jewish state.

This difference of opinion about what Israel means to the Jews was one of the first conflicts between the two groups. More important differences emerged in terms of education, employment, and political power. Many Sephardim were unable to read or write, and the only jobs open to them were low-paying construction and laborer positions. Most of the country's top government positions were filled by Ashkenazim.

Within a few years after Israel's creation, the Sephardim formed the majority of Israel's population. But they were still treated as outsiders. This partly resulted from the segregation of the Sephardim from the Ashkenazim. When the first Sephardic immigrants arrived, the government placed them in rural areas and less-populated communities. Whole towns and cities became Sephardic as a result.

Only after the Six-Day War in 1967 did the divisions between the Sephardim and the Ashkenazim heal somewhat. Many Sephardim fought and died in the war, and the Ashkenazim recognized the Sephardic sacrifice for the state of Israel. However, even today the Sephardim are, on average, poorer than the Ashkenazim and still do not hold powerful positions in government. The conflict between the two groups will continue until the Sephardim believe they are equal partners of the Ashkenazim.

Religious Conflict

Since independence, Israelis have argued about what it means to call Israel a Jewish state. Does it mean only that it is home for all people who call themselves Jews? Or does it mean that Israel should be governed according to the laws and rituals of the Jewish religion?

Orthodox Jews (Jews who live in strict accordance with the halakah, the laws of Judaism) want Israeli society to function according to these biblical laws. In their view, Israel should be a theocracy, a country where there is no separation between government and religion. Opposing this extreme position are secular (nonreligious) Jews, who do not believe that Jewish beliefs should govern everyday life for all Jews. Disagreement between these two groups has led to violent, bloody confrontations. The conflict over just how Jewish Israel should be is one of the most serious issues facing the country.

Orthodox Jews make up only a small portion of the population. They live in their own neighborhoods and wear distinctive clothing: men and boys dress in black hats and suits with prayer shawls called *tzitzit* wrapped around their waists and style their hair in long side curls called *pais;* women and girls wear long, simple dresses and headscarves.

Secular Jews make up the majority of the population and have prevented the Orthodox Jews from creating a theocracy. But many of the Orthodox Jews' beliefs have become civil law. For example, Sabbath day, which runs from sundown Friday to sundown Saturday, is strictly observed in Israel. No Israeli aircraft may fly, no ship may enter or leave Israeli ports, and, if the local authorities agree, no public transportation, restaurants, or entertainment facilities may open.

The Orthodox Jews have also been able to ban civil marriage and divorce. Since 1953, the law has required all Jewish Israelis to marry or divorce in religious courts, which are administered by rabbis and watched over by the government's Ministry of Religious Affairs.

The Orthodox also want the government to adopt the Orthodox definition of who is a Jew. According to the Orthodox, a "true" Jew is someone whose mother is Jewish or someone who has converted to Judaism through an approved Orthodox authority. This restrictive definition is a particularly bitter issue among the children of converted parents. It would have a strong effect on the Law of Return, which grants citizenship to Jews who immigrate to Israel. If the Orthodox definition of who is a Jew became law, many converted

Jews and others who fall outside the definition's limits would be barred from citizenship.

About 6 percent of the Orthodox are known as ultra-Orthodox Jews because their views are even more extreme than those of the Orthodox. The ultra-Orthodox believe that they have the right to throw stones at Israelis who drive cars on the Sabbath, to attack government officials with whom they disagree, and to strike Christian women who wear clothing they consider immodest. On religious holidays such as Yom Kippur, when religious law prohibits almost any activity, including eating or drinking, the ultra-Orthodox may react violently when they observe action or behavior that they perceive as desecration of the holiness of the day.

Secular Jews resent being told who is a Jew and who is not, and they do not accept the Orthodox restrictions placed on their freedoms. But the Orthodox have great political power despite their small numbers, making it doubtful that the secular Jews will be able to make any major changes.

Arab laborers in Israel wear their colorful headdresses, called kaffiyehs, *while working.*

The Arabs of Israel

About 920,000 Arabs live in Israel. Israeli Arabs are the descendants of the Palestinians who lived in what is now Israel for more than 1,000 years. When Israel became independent, more than 400,000 Palestinians left, many moving to the West Bank or to Lebanon. Those who remained in Israel were placed under military rule until 1966, when they received most of the same political and legal rights as Israeli Jews. The more than 2.75 million Palestinians who live in the Israeli-occupied West Bank and Gaza Strip do not share these rights. Since 1995, however, Palestinians in these territories have had the right to participate in elections for membership in the Palestinian Council, a self-governing body.

In their years under Israeli rule, the Israeli Arabs' health care, education, and housing have improved somewhat. However, in comparison with the overall Israeli population, Israeli Arabs have lower paying jobs and poorer housing and medical care. Moreover, even though they have the right to vote, Israeli Arabs have not been able to form effective political parties that would give them a voice in governing the country. Some Arabs do serve in the Israeli Knesset (parliament), however.

A wide gulf divides Arabs and Jews in Israel. Jews and Arabs live in different neighborhoods, attend different primary schools, and usually do not intermarry. Israel's Arabs have occasionally been the targets of terrorist attacks by Jewish militants, and many complain that ethnic discrimination and segregation are widespread. There has been some mixing of cultures (for example, Israeli menus include many Arab dishes), but division will continue until the many complex issues that divide Israelis and Arabs are resolved.

An Israeli girl (center) teaches Hebrew to a group of Ethiopian children whose families have emigrated to Israel. Many Jews who come to Israel from other parts of the world need help learning the language and customs of their new home.

A Vibrant Democracy

Israel is a democratic republic with a parliamentary form of government. The president, the prime minister and his cabinet (together called the "government"), and the Knesset, or parliament, share governmental responsibility.

The head of state is the president of the republic. Elected by a majority vote of the Knesset, the president may serve no more than two consecutive five-year terms. The president's role is chiefly ceremonial. He represents the nation at important events and, on the advice of the Knesset, appoints judges, concludes treaties, receives foreign diplomats, and signs bills into law. Israel's first president was Chaim Weizmann, a leading figure in the Zionist movement.

The prime minister acts as the head of government and exercises executive power. Although the prime minister is officially appointed by the president, the actual selection is made beforehand by political party leaders in the Knesset. The prime minister oversees a cabinet made up of various government ministers.

Supreme governmental authority rests with the third branch, the Knesset. This single-chamber body has 120 members who are elected to four-year terms in national elections. Voters, who must be at least 18 years old, do not select individual candidates; rather, they choose a list of men and women from one of Israel's political parties. The percentage of the total vote won by the party determines the number of seats the party will receive in the Knesset. This method of selecting members is called proportional representation.

The Knesset sets the government's budget and oversees budget matters through the office of the comptroller of state (whom the Knesset appoints). The government is responsible to the Knesset; that is, the Knesset can vote to dissolve the government when a majority of Knesset members lose confidence in the policies of the prime minister and his cabinet.

Israel's judicial system has both civil and religious courts. The highest civil court in the land is the Supreme Court, which exercises power over the religious courts in some matters. Five district courts, 29 magistrates' courts, 4 labor courts, and juvenile and municipal courts round out the civil court system. Israel has a very low crime rate and one of the world's lowest rates of homicide.

Separate religious courts are under the jurisdiction of the Jewish, Muslim, Christian, and Druze communities. Religious courts oversee matters such as marriage, divorce, alimony, and religious wills. Judgments are based on the tenets of the faith involved.

Israel is divided into six administrative districts: Northern, Haifa, Central, Jerusalem, Tel Aviv, and Southern. A commissioner appointed by the central government heads each district. The commissioner reports to the minister of the interior.

Israel's 33 cities and 9 smaller towns are governed locally by either municipal corporations, local councils, or regional councils, which are set up in agricultural areas. The occupied West Bank and Gaza Strip are administered by civil authorities under the jurisdiction of the popularly elected Palestinian Council.

Israel has no written constitution or bill of rights. Since 1950, however, the Knesset has decided that certain laws should be part of a future constitution. Israelis have the right to assemble, to petition the government, to form unions, to bargain collectively, and to strike. The privacy of one's home, mail, and telephone are protected by law, as are the freedom of worship and the freedom of speech. But all books, television programs, movies, plays, and newspapers must go before a military censor, who looks for material that might undermine national security.

Education

Israel's founders made free education a cornerstone of the state. The early Zionist settlers established schools in the late 19th century, when Palestine was governed by the Turks. Immediately after Israel gained independence, the government began to build schools with the same enthusiasm with which it constructed roads, houses, and agricultural settlements. Today, about 8 percent of the government's annual budget is spent on education.

Every child between the ages of 6 and 16 is required to attend school. The school system is organized into kindergarten, six-year

Every child between the ages of 6 and 16 is required to attend school, which is free.

TEL AVIV UNIVERSIT
MATATIA GATE

Tel Aviv University, founded in 1956, has schools of law, humanities, science, medicine, and social work.

primary schools, three-year junior secondary schools, and three-year secondary schools. At the end of their schooling, Israeli students take a comprehensive examination to determine whether they can attend college.

The government operates three types of schools: religious schools for Jews; secular state schools (that is, schools with no religious affiliation); and state schools for Arabs. In addition, Orthodox and ultra-Orthodox Jews operate their own schools, which are supervised by the state to ensure that they meet national standards.

Israeli students study the history of the world and their country; languages (usually English and French); mathematics; sciences; and literature. Most Israeli children enjoy school, and very few drop out. The quality of education is very high, and parents encourage their children to be good students. Most Israelis are high-school graduates, and many attend college after military service.

Israel has several universities with excellent reputations. One of them is Hebrew University, which is located on Mount Scopus in East Jerusalem. The university, which provides education in all the major disciplines, has 15 schools. It has 1,400 senior faculty members and nearly 23,000 full-time students.

Tel Aviv University, founded in 1956, has nine faculties, 106 departments, and over 75 research institutes. The Israel Institute of Technology (Technion), known worldwide primarily for its engineering curriculum, also features a medical faculty and a nautical school. Other major universities include Bar-Ilan University, which offers a wide range of courses to over 20,000 students; the Israel Institute of Technology in Haifa; and the Weizmann Institute of Science in Rehobot. Palestinian institutions of higher education include An-Najah National University in Nablus, with an enrollment of about 7,000 students, and BirZeit University in Ramallah.

Staying Healthy

The quality of Israeli medical and dental care is comparable to the health care provided in Europe and the United States. There are more than 27,000 physicians in the country, giving Israel an average of one doctor for every 200 people, one of the highest ratios in the world. The average life expectancy of Jewish males is 75.9 years; for Jewish females, 79.7 years. (Life expectancy among Arabs is lower: 73.8 years for males and 77.1 years for females.)

All Israeli infants are vaccinated, and most childhood diseases are under control. But among adults, heart disease and cancer account for two-thirds of the deaths. A high percentage of the population smokes, including 35 percent of high school seniors and juniors, despite recent anti-smoking campaigns by the government.

The government sets high standards for health care. It requires that at least one pharmacy in a neighborhood be open or on call at all times. However, during Yom Kippur medical care also falls victim to the country's holiest holiday, and even ambulance drivers and attendants may refuse to work.

A Diversity of Views

Politics is a passionate issue in Israel. Political debates between Israelis can be heard on many streetcorners. Among politicians emotions run high and violence is not unknown: at the Herut party convention in 1985, angry party members threw chairs at each other. And debates about especially volatile issues have caused fistfights in the Knesset.

The Israelis' intense political passions have led them to form many political parties. The number of parties shows the liveliness of Israeli democracy: whereas most democratic countries have only two or three parties that play a leading role in the government, a dozen or more parties typically have seats in the Israeli Knesset. And political parties in Israel do more than elect legislators. Almost every party publishes its own newspaper, and many sponsor social events, provide medical services, or run sports organizations.

The multitude of political parties means that many views are represented. The most important parties are Labor and Likud. The smaller parties are divided into several groupings: national-religious, ultra-orthodox religious, centrist, left-wing, nationalist, immigrant, and Arab parties. In recent elections, Labor and Likud together won just over half the seats in the Knesset, and the small parties increased in strength. But none of these small parties receives over 10 percent of the vote.

The social-democratic Labor party has a long history in Israel. Formed by early Ashkenazic immigrants, it played a major role in the government of early 20th-century Palestine. All of Israel's leaders were Labor party members until the election of Menachem Begin of the Likud in 1977.

The major difference between Likud and Labor is in policy on the Occupied Territories. A key part of the Likud platform concerns the fate of Jewish settlement in the Gaza Strip and the West Bank, areas that Likud calls by the biblical names Judea and Samaria. These areas, Likud believes, should remain under full Israeli control. Likud also stresses a free-market economy, in contrast to Labor's advocacy of a more prominent role of government in economic affairs.

Because no party has been able to capture a majority of seats in the Knesset, Israeli governments have been coalitions in which one party with a large number of seats wins support from smaller parties and divides up the government ministries. This arrangement failed in 1984, when neither Labor nor Likud could gain enough support among the small parties to form a coalition. At that point, despite their significant differences on policy, the two parties agreed on a broad-based "government of national unity." Under the agreement, the prime minister's post was passed in mid-term from Labor to Likud.

Israeli election law was changed prior to the 1996 elections, providing that separate ballots be cast for prime minister and Knesset members. Benjamin Netanyahu of Likud was the first prime minister to be elected under the new law, and his party formed the coalition government in the Knesset.

With so many parties and so many different points of view, it is easy to think that Israel's government has always been in disarray. This has not been the case. Israel's leaders have often proved able and willing to take bold, sometimes controversial, steps to move their country forward.

The Burden of Defense

After four major wars and countless terrorist attacks, it is not surprising that the Israeli Defense Force plays an important role in

Israeli society. Israel spends as much as $9.2 billion a year on defense. Although much of this money comes in the form of loans and grants from the United States, large defense expenditures have created enormous strains on the government's budget. As a result, Israeli citizens pay some of the highest taxes in the world.

Israel's armed services, called the Israeli Defense Forces (IDF), consist of ground forces, an air force, and a navy. Made up of career personnel and conscripts, the full-time standing army is relatively small and focused on providing early-warning capability. Most of the army's forces are reservists who participate regularly in training. In time of war, these reservists can quickly be mobilized. With the exception of Orthodox Jewish women and Arabs, all Israelis, including Druze, must serve in the IDF.

Drafted men serve in the IDF for three years, women for 21

Women as well as men are drafted into the Israeli military, usually when they are 18. Few women participate in combat, however.

months. Deferments may be granted for students at institutions of higher education. Depending on their age and personal status when entering the country, new immigrants may gain deferments for a short period of time.

After satisfying requirements for compulsory service, all Israeli soldiers remain in the IDF as reservists. They continue to train on a regular basis until age 51 for men and age 24 for unmarried women. Reservists serve 39 days a year in training, and they remain for longer periods in times of emergency. The country's policy is to reduce the need for reserve service when possible, and reservists who have served in combat units may be discharged at age 45.

The Israeli army is well trained, but it is also extremely casual. Officers and conscripts consider each other equals, and discipline is loose. Uniforms are unkempt, and many men have beards and long hair. Marching in step, parades, and elaborate military ceremonies are unheard of.

Soldiers are everywhere in Israel: in supermarkets, with their Uzi machine guns resting in their shopping carts alongside groceries; at bus stops, waiting patiently with other riders; or at sidewalk cafes, their guns cradled in their laps as they sip coffee. Israelis do not feel threatened by this constant military presence because they believe the soldiers guarantee their security. Tanks and other armored vehicles sometimes crowd the highways and create traffic jams, but there is little horn-honking or complaining by civilian drivers.

Surprisingly, the IDF's presence everywhere in Israel does not mean that the IDF has a direct role in the government or in politics (except in the occupied territories). Military leaders recognize that they are under the command of the Israeli government.

Tel Aviv's skyline points up the city's role as the center of Israel's commercial and cultural life.

A Changing Economy

Israel's economic growth since its independence has been impressive. In 1948, the tiny nation seemed to face a bleak future: the Arab states had prohibited trade with Israel, hundreds of thousands of unskilled immigrants were flowing into the country, food had to be rationed, housing was inadequate, and a huge defense budget left little money for government investment in the economy.

Today, Israelis enjoy a standard of living equal to that of people in Italy and Great Britain. Almost all Israelis live in comfortable homes, most foods are plentiful, and many Israelis possess the same types of cars, televisions, and washing machines that people in other Western countries own.

But economic growth does not mean that Israel has solved all its economic problems. Though it has made some breakthroughs in trade with its Arab neighbors, that commerce is still very limited. The country still lacks significant natural resources or domestic energy sources. In addition, the defense budget and the burden of absorbing immigrants put strains on the economy.

Israel's economic growth relies in large part on outside investment and aid from three important sources: the United States, war reparations from Germany, and donations from Jews living outside

Israel. Of course, the resourcefulness and hard work of Israelis have also been important.

Israel's gross domestic product or GDP—the total of all goods and services produced in the country—reached $80 billion by 1995. Public services (those provided by the government) account for 33 percent of the GDP; commercial services, such as hotels, restaurants, banking, and tourism, 27 percent; industry, 22 percent; transportation and communications, 8 percent; construction, 7 percent; and agriculture, 3 percent.

Because Israel has so few natural resources, it depends heavily on imports, especially oil for energy production and raw materials for industry. The high prices of these items (especially oil) leave Israel with a large trade deficit—that is, it imports many more goods than it exports, so it spends more than it earns in trade with other countries. The large trade deficit continues to worry the government.

Agriculture

Agriculture employs around 3 percent of Israel's working population, and contributes only 3 percent of the national income. Nevertheless, it plays a large role in Israeli culture and history. Early Zionist settlers worked the land on settlements called kibbutzim (farms on which everyone shares in the work). Swamps were drained and desert lands irrigated through enormous expenditures of human labor.

Today, over 1 million acres (413,000 hectares) are under cultivation. Much of this land has to be irrigated. For this reason, most of the country's fresh-water sources have been joined in the National Water Carrier, which transfers water from the north to the agricultural areas of the semi-arid south.

Major agricultural crops include vegetables, cotton, beef, poultry and dairy products, and citrus and other fruits. Citrus fruits are the country's main export crop. Israel's soil and climate give the fruit an appearance and flavor that command a high price on the world market.

Industry

Industrial progress has had a large impact on the Israeli economy. Israel's rate of industrial output growth, 32.5 percent, was second only to Korea's among Western societies in the first half of the 1990s. Today, industry employs over a fifth of Israel's workers.

The area around Haifa, in northwestern Israel, is home to most of Israel's heavy industry. Petroleum refineries, foundries, a steel mill, an automobile assembly plant, chemical plants, and tire and fertilizer factories are found in the region.

Many light industries, such as food processing and textile manufacturing, are located in and around Tel Aviv. Jerusalem has shoe manufacturers, printing plants, and pencil factories. Plants for cutting and polishing diamonds, which by the mid-1990s accounted for $4.6 billion in Israeli exports, are located north of Tel Aviv.

The most significant industrial growth has occurred in the high-technology sectors, which accounted for over six-tenths of the industrial product in recent years. Almost half of this output is exported, providing about two-thirds of total industrial exports.

A Stable Future?

Israelis now enjoy relative economic security. After a peak in unemployment in the early 1990s, the jobless rate dropped below 7 percent. Inflation, though still higher than in most Western countries, remains bearable.

The government's 1985 economic stabilization program is the major reason for this stability. In the early 1980s, the Israeli economy suffered from large price increases (inflation). The government's budget was in deficit, and the *shekel,* Israel's unit of currency, had become almost worthless.

The Labor and Likud coalition government rescued the shekel by issuing a new currency called the New Israeli shekel (1 new shekel is divided into 100 agorot). Sharp reductions in the government budget and an initiative to privatize state-owned enterprises led to decreased inflation and reasonable economic growth. Today, the economy grows at an annual rate of between 5 and 7 percent.

Still, Israeli families find that they spend the greatest portion of their paychecks on everyday items that are expensive because they have to be imported. Food (especially beef and fish), and gasoline, and clothing all must be imported from other countries.

The cutbacks in the government's budget have restricted the amount of money that can be spent on social welfare needs such as

More than 1 million acres are under cultivation, but most of this land has to be irrigated.

health care and housing. However, most Israelis seem willing to accept these cuts in government social spending if they mean a better economic future.

Transportation

Israel has an excellent transportation network of highways and railroads. There are 8,365 miles (13,460 kilometers) of highways in the country, virtually all of which are paved and well marked in both Hebrew and English. Many Israelis own cars and prefer to travel by automobile, though a considerable number of them are killed and injured each year in traffic accidents. Israelis have a reputation for fast and sometimes reckless driving.

Passengers and freight travel over the country's 340 miles (516 kilometers) of railway line. Although more people are riding trains, they remain the least popular means of transportation. Tourists may enjoy the trip by rail between Tel Aviv and Jerusalem because it passes through many biblical sites, but most Israelis prefer to drive the same route.

Ben-Gurion Airport is the largest airport in the country. About 2,400 international flights land in Israel each year, bringing more than 3.7 million passengers. The national airline, El Al ("up and away" in Hebrew), has its headquarters at Ben-Gurion Airport.

Three Israeli towns have commercial ports: Haifa, Elat, and Ashdod. Each year, a total of 5,400 ships dock at these ports to transport the imports and exports that are so vital to Israel's economy.

The Media

Israel's communications facilities—including the post office, and the telephone, telegraph, and broadcasting services—are owned by the government. The eight radio networks of *Kol Yisrael* (Voice of Israel) offer programming in 17 languages, and the Israeli television networks broadcast a full range of programs, including popular American comedies and dramas.

Newspapers play an important role in the country's political life. Most Hebrew-language morning papers are affiliated with a political party or religious organization. The two most important daily papers are *Ha'aretz* (The Land) and *Davar* (The Word), both of which are published in Tel Aviv. No newspapers are published on Saturday, because rules prohibit publishing on the Sabbath.

Israelis typically pause in their work at noon to go home or to relax in cafes.

Living in Israel

Israel is one of the few countries in the world whose population is spread evenly throughout the land. When immigrants began arriving in huge numbers after 1948, the government decided to resettle them in towns spread across Israel. Not all immigrants were happy about this decision, because many wanted to live in the larger cities with other immigrants from their countries. This policy contributed to conflict between the Ashkenazim and the Sephardim. Today, Israelis may live wherever they choose.

The nation's 30 cities and 70 towns share the rhythm of the typical Israeli day. At noon, when the overhead sun is at its hottest, work stops. Men and women leave their jobs to go home, or to sit and relax in cafes. Older Arab men sit in the town squares and finger their worry beads, pushing their headdresses back as they lean over to make a point to a friend. Everything is quiet, and a rare moment of peace prevails.

At four o'clock work resumes. The traffic becomes heavy again, and the noise and bustle return until seven o'clock in the evening, when most businesses close for the day. But work never stops on the nation's agricultural settlements, which are a unique feature of life in Israel.

The Kibbutzniks

A kibbutz is a cooperative settlement devoted to farming and governed by its members. There are some 270 kibbutzim (the plural of kibbutz) in Israel. They attract volunteers from around the world. A kibbutz can have more than 1,000 members or as few as 40. The state leases land to kibbutzniks (the people who live on the kibbutz) for 49 years, at which time the lease can be renewed. Although the proportion of Israelis who live on kibbutzim has declined, the principles of kibbutz life still influence the nation.

The original kibbutzim were founded by the early Zionist settlers. Many of these settlers had worked in industry, medicine, or

Two men harvest the crop in a kibbutz, or cooperative farm.

education in Europe, but believed that returning to Israel required a change in life-style. The Zionist ideal was to abandon the Old World pressure for material success and to "return to the land" and live a simple life. Because the Zionists believed in socialism and thought that all goods and property should be collectively held, the self-governing kibbutz became the cornerstone of the Zionist hopes for Israel.

A kibbutz's funds, land, equipment, stock, and buildings are owned by all the kibbutzniks. Committees and officers elected by the kibbutzniks decide how the kibbutz's income will be distributed. Jobs are rotated, so that a kibbutznik will work at planting for part of the year, then move on to kitchen or administrative work—whatever job is necessary to keep the kibbutz running. Kibbutzniks do not receive salaries. In most businesses this would cause people to avoid working, but kibbutzniks know that their individual efforts provide better lives for all. Anyone who does not do his or her share of the work on the kibbutz is soon asked to leave.

Kibbutzniks eat together in a communal dining hall that is much like a school cafeteria. Married kibbutzniks live in small houses, whereas single people and volunteers share small cottages. The kibbutz provides each kibbutznik with clothing, usually dark blue shirts and shorts or pants.

In some kibbutzim, mothers and fathers tend to their own children, but in others children are cared for by many adult kibbutzniks. Children eat, sleep, and study in their own rooms, separate from the adults. Responsibilities come at an early age: children have jobs and their own fields and crops to tend. The children attend kibbutz schools that meet national standards but are independent of the state-run school system.

Kibbutzniks have always been treated with great respect by other Israelis. For many years they were thought of as the "conscience" of the country, people who put aside material values in order to work the land and share their wealth. Kibbutzniks also had a heroic appeal in Israel's early days because they were often the first line of defense against the Arab armies; men, women, and children all shouldered guns to protect their new nation.

In recent years, however, the image of the kibbutz has changed. As the proportion of national income derived from agriculture has declined, virtually all kibbutzim have expanded into various kinds of industry, particularly metal work, plastics, and processed foods. Kibbutzim have also become centers of tourism, with a broad array of recreational facilities for both Israelis and foreign visitors. Many regret these developments as departures from the values that defined the kibbutz spirit. Others believe that the ability to change with the broader Israeli society is a key to the kibbutz's survival.

Tel Aviv

Tel Aviv is the largest city in Israel. With a population of more than 2.5 million, it encompasses the medieval city of Jaffa and surrounding suburbs. Founded in 1908 as the first Jewish settlement in Palestine, it has grown into a modern, 20th-century city dominated by office and apartment buildings.

Located in the middle of Israel's Mediterranean coast, Tel Aviv is the center of Israel's commercial and cultural life. More than 50 percent of all Israeli industry is located here, as are the Israeli stock exchange and most large corporations. Almost all foreign embassies are also located here, because many nations recognize Tel Aviv and not Jerusalem as Israel's capital. Many nations claim that Jerusalem should return to the international status planned for it by the United Nations in 1947.

Movie theaters, nightclubs, discos, restaurants, and sidewalk cafes border the city's busy, noisy streets. Tourists crowd the white, sandy beaches and swim in the warm, clear blue waters of the Mediterranean.

Within an hour's walk from Tel Aviv's beaches is the old city of Jaffa. Once an ancient port city, it now stands studded with the ruins of ancient fortifications dating from 1300 B.C. The city's narrow streets carry shoppers to the heart of the Jaffa flea market, where dozens of shops sell everything from used jeans to menorahs (candelabra used for Jewish worship).

Sixty miles north of Tel Aviv-Jaffa is the busy port city of Haifa. Halfway up the road to Haifa stand the remains of Caesarea, a city built by King Herod in honor of the Roman emperor Caesar Augustus. A large amphitheater is now the major attraction; here 2,000 Jews were publicly executed for staging a revolt against their Roman rulers in 66 A.D. North of the amphitheater are the remains of a fort built by Crusaders 1,000 years ago.

The Holy City

In Hebrew it is called *Yerushalayim shel ma'alah* — "Heavenly City." For three religions it is the most sacred spot on earth. To Jews it has been the symbol of national and religious freedom since King David captured it in the 10th century B.C. To Christians it is the place where Jesus Christ lived, taught, and was crucified. And to Muslims, it is the site from which Muhammad rose into heaven, and to which he will return on Judgment Day.

Archaeological remains found in Jerusalem show that cave dwellers occupied the area around 3500 B.C. The name Jerusalem first appeared in Egyptian writings around 1900 B.C., and there are records of a Jerusalemite king named Abdi-Hiba, who ruled the area around 1360 B.C. After King David conquered Jerusalem for the Hebrews, it became known as the "City of David."

King Solomon, David's successor, enlarged the city and made it the headquarters of his business ventures and trading schemes. Most important, he built the magnificent First Temple here. Jerusalem suffered terrible destruction in 598 B.C. when the Babylonians razed the city walls, demolished the Temple, and burned down all the houses and palaces. The Jews rebuilt the city and the temple in 538 B.C.

King Herod, the puppet ruler installed by Rome, made many improvements to the city. The Wailing Wall, which is revered today as the holiest of all Jewish shrines, was actually built by the half-Jewish Herod to shore up the crumbling western wall of the Second Temple. The old king's improvements were demolished by the Romans during the Zealot rebellion in 70 A.D.

In 325 A.D., the Byzantine emperor Constantine declared Jerusalem a Christian city. Pagan temples and altars were destroyed.

The Wailing Wall is revered today as the holiest of Jewish shrines.

The tomb where Jesus Christ had been buried was excavated. In the 11th century the Crusaders enshrined the site in a basilica. The basilica is known today as the Church of the Holy Sepulchre.

In 638, Islamic armies swept into Jerusalem. These Muslims added to the city's religious monuments, building the Dome of the Rock mosque on a huge rock formation overlooking the Temple site. It was here, Muslims believe, that Mohammed rose to heaven.

Jerusalem continued to change hands until 1517, when it was captured by the Ottoman Turkish Empire. The Ottomans held the city until the end of World War I, when the British took control.

Today, Jerusalem is actually two cities: the ancient walled city, and the modern "new" city that the Jews call *Yerushalayim shel matah*—"everyday Jerusalem." New Jerusalem is neither mystical nor particularly special. Construction of the city began in 1860, after Jewish immigrants built a suburb to the west of the old city. Mea Shearim, an area where Orthodox Jews live, is in the new city, as are the Knesset, the Israel Museum, and many restaurants and schools. Building regulations require most housing to be constructed only out of locally quarried limestone, called Jerusalem stone. This gives the new city, with its forests of television antennas, buses, cars, and nondescript suburbs, an older, more attractive look.

New Jerusalem's hills are steep and rocky. In the evenings, the aroma of wild flowers growing in gardens and hillsides fills the air. City dwellers call the fragrance "Jerusalem Perfume" and it lasts until dawn, when the sun burns off the fragrance. On Sabbath nights men can be heard chanting melodic Hebrew prayers inside their synagogues, and the streets are filled with Orthodox Jews in their distinctive black clothing.

Until 1967, Jerusalem was a divided city. Israel claimed new Jerusalem, and the neighboring kingdom of Jordan held the old city. But during the Six-Day War in 1967, the Israeli Defense Force captured the old city from the Jordanians. When the fighting ended,

Israeli soldiers raced to the Wailing Wall for an emotional reunion with a symbol of their religion.

Four quarters, or sections, are contained within the city's walls: the Jewish Quarter, once a ghetto but now rebuilt with elegant condominium apartments; the Christian Quarter, where the Church of the Holy Sepulchre is located; the Armenian Quarter, behind whose many doors are lovely religious retreats and chapels; and the Muslim Quarter, which includes the ancient temple area.

The old city also contains a typical Arab *suq*, or bazaar, tightly packed with tiny shops selling trinkets, clothing, and souvenirs. The suq is filled with the odors of lamb cooking, incense burning, coffee steaming, and animal hides drying in the sunlight.

East Jerusalem is the largest Arab neighborhood in the city. Jews live here with the Arab population, eating in Arab restaurants, shopping in Arab markets and stores, and buying the hot, soft sesame rolls and breads Arab merchants sell on the street.

The old city of Jerusalem is a special place. Lit by spotlights at night, the massive wall that surrounds the city glows pale and mysterious. It is impossible for a visitor to forget that this holy city has cradled three of the world's great religions.

The West Bank

The old city of Jerusalem is located on the West Bank, a strip of territory that was won from Jordan during the Six-Day War. Called the West Bank because it is on the West side of the Jordan River, the status of this slice of territory has become the most controversial issue in Israel. About 1.5 million Palestinians live here. Israel has not annexed the territory (made it part of Israel), but its future political status remains in doubt.

Since 1977, thousands of young Israeli Jews have moved into the West Bank to take advantage of government-built, low-cost housing. These Israeli settlements have created a furor among the Palestinians living in the West Bank and among Israelis, who are divided on whether the settlements should be built. Rock throwing by young Palestinians has been met by Israeli gunfire, and random terrorism by both Palestinian and Jewish terrorists keeps the area in a constant state of tension.

What to do with the West Bank remains perhaps the most difficult question facing Israel. The recent beginnings of Palestinian self-government have offered some hope of resolution, but many obstacles remain to be overcome.

The Israeli Defense Force has become one of the world's most lethal armies.

Things to Remember

Israel is a nation born of conflict. War began immediately on its independence, and later wars and continuing terrorist violence have forced Israelis to value the security of their state above any other considerations.

Today, half a century after its declaration of independence, Israel's survival as an independent Jewish state seems ensured. The Israeli Defense Forces have become one of the world's strongest armies. Moreover, courageous peace initiatives such as the 1979 Israel-Egypt peace treaty and negotiations arising from a 1991 peace conference in Madrid show that fear and distrust need not be the only emotions shared by Israel and its Arab neighbors. Peace and trust are also possible.

The resolve with which Israel confronted its neighbors has been matched inside Israel. A relatively strong economy and a functioning democratic government are two achievements that many other young independent countries have yet to find. People who are almost all immigrants from other lands have worked to create living and educational standards equivalent to those in Western countries.

Standing alongside these achievements are serious problems that have yet to be solved: the ongoing trade deficit, religious and

The central issue facing Israel remains the conflict with thousands of Palestinian Arabs like this man. These Arabs claim lands held by Israel as their homeland.

ethnic differences, and continuing difficulties in addressing Palestinian demands for a homeland.

Israel must learn to live without massive amounts of foreign aid. Its economy has grown with the hard work and determination of its people, but the most important fuel has been money from the United States and from Jews living outside the country. The development of industry and services may free Israel from this shackle on its economic development.

The divisions between religious and nonreligious Jews will no doubt continue, but a reasonable solution to their differing views of Israel will require moderation and negotiation, especially on the part of the Orthodox Jews. The ethnic conflict between Oriental and European Jews will heal with time, however, as Oriental Jews begin to assume positions of power in business and government.

Perhaps the chief issue facing Israel is the resolution of what is called the "Palestinian problem." Whether Israelis can come together to work out a solution to this challenge is the central question. Many Israelis bear the scars of past conflicts with the Arabs. Many would like to annex the West Bank and the Gaza Strip. There have been both breakthroughs and setbacks in recent years in coming to terms with the Palestinians. Much difficult work remains to be done to achieve a lasting peace.

Former prime minister David Ben-Gurion, shown speaking at the Waldorf Astoria in New York City in 1951, is remembered by Israelis as a warrior for independence.

◄GLOSSARY►

aliyah   Hebrew for return; Jews who immigrate to Israel are said to make aliyah.

Ashkenazim   Israeli Jews of European descent.

babaganoush   A dip made from roasted eggplant, spices, and tahini.

Balfour Declaration   The British government's 1917 approval of the Zionist movement's plea to allow Jews to live in Palestine.

Bedouins   Arabs who live as nomads.

Canaan   The ancient name for what has now become the state of Israel. The inhabitants of Canaan were called Canaanites.

Diaspora   Derived from the Greek for "to be dispersed." Jews forced into exile from Palestine after the Romans destroyed Jerusalem were said to be in the Diaspora.

Druze   A group that split from the Islamic movement around 996. The Druze allow no conversions or marriage with outsiders; their religious practices are secretive and shrouded in mysticism.

falafel   A spicy vegetable mixture that is rolled into balls, fried, and made into sandwiches with pita bread.

habiru   The Canaanites who inhabited Israel called the first Jews to enter Canaan habiru, which means "wanderers." Over time, the word evolved into "Hebrew."

Holocaust Nazi Germany's extermination of almost six million Jews during Adolf Hitler's reign.

hummus A paste made with mashed chickpeas, lemon, garlic, and tahini.

IDF The Israeli Defense Force; the name given to Israel's military forces.

kibbutz A cooperative agricultural settlement; the members of the kibbutz (called kibbutzniks) share equally in all the work and in any profits made from the farmwork. The kibbutz plays a central role in Israel's early history.

Knesset The Israeli parliament.

leban A slightly sour yogurt that can be served plain or with fruit flavoring.

Muslim A follower of Islam.

Occupied Territories The West Bank and the Gaza Strip, which were taken over by Israel during the Six-Day War but have not been formally annexed.

October War The fourth major war Israel fought with the surrounding Arab nations; Egypt and Syria launched surprise attacks on Israel in October 1973, but Israel was able to beat back the Arab advances. Also called the Yom Kippur War by most Israelis.

Orthodox Jew A Jew who strictly follows the halakah, a body of religious laws governing Jewish behavior.

pita bread Flat bread baked in hollow, small circular loaves.

Promised Land According to the Bible, the land of Israel was promised to the Hebrews, God's "chosen people," after the Hebrews made a covenant (agreement) with God.

Sephardim Jews descended from people living in the Near East and the Mediterranean basin; many immigrated to Israel in the early years after independence. They are also called Oriental Jews.

service industry A term economists use to refer to work that does not create actual products like those created in factories; hotels, restaurants, and computer sales are examples of service industries.

shwarma Thin slices of cooked, spicy lamb stuffed into pita bread.

Six-Day War The third major war Israel fought with its Arab neighbors; Israeli forces destroyed the Arab air forces and overran the Sinai Peninsula, the Golan Heights, east Jerusalem, the Gaza Strip, and the West Bank in six days in June, 1967.

tahini Sesame paste added to hummus and mixed with lemon juice, garlic, and salt; the tahini is spread inside the pita bread.

Temple The name used to refer to the successive synagogues built in Jerusalem. The most important temple was the First Temple, which was built by King Solomon.

theocracy A state governed by religious precepts.

Yom Kippur The holiest Jewish religious holiday, the Day of Atonement.

Zealots A Jewish guerrilla group that led a rebellion against the Roman occupation of Israel in 70 A.D.; the Zealots committed mass suicide at the fortress of Masada rather than surrender to the Romans.

Zionism The movement begun by European Jews to create a home for the Jews of the world. The Zionists believed in socialism, and hoped to build a Socialist society in Israel.

PICTURE CREDITS

‹ I N D E X ›